Test Your Professional English

Accounting

Alison Pohl

Series Editor: Nick Brieger

PENGUIN ENGLISH

For Thomas and Johanna

Pearson Education Limited
Edinburgh Gate
Harlow
Essex CM20 2JE, England
and Associated Companies throughout the world.

ISBN 0 582 45163 9

First published 1997 under the title *Test Your Business English: Accounting*
This edition published 2002

Designed and typeset by Pantek Arts Ltd, Maidstone, Kent
Test Your format devised by Peter Watcyn-Jones
Illustrations by David Eaton, Anthony Seldon and Vince Silcock
Printed in Italy by Rotolito Lombarda

Acknowledgements
I wish to extend my grateful thanks to Philip Triffitt and Helmut Pohl for providing material and support with this book. As always, grateful thanks are also due to our series editor, Nick Brieger, and to the team at Penguin Longman.

Published by Pearson Education Limited in association with Penguin Books Ltd, both companies being subsidiaries of Pearson plc.

Contents

To the student

Do you use English in your work or as part of your studies? You may be a professional accountant, a student or have an interest in accounting as part of your job. Whatever your background, the tests in this book will help you improve your knowledge of accountancy terms in English. They cover all the most important vocabulary and expressions to really help you communicate more effectively and confidently when working in English.

The book has been divided into eight sections. The first section is an introduction to general accountancy terms and concepts. The other seven sections deal with important topic areas in the the field of financial accounting and management accounting including business organization, costing, and financial statements and ratios. You may choose to work through the book from beginning to end or may find it more useful to select tests according to your interests and needs.

Many tests also have tips (advice) on language, language learning and professional information. Do read these explanations and tips: they are there to help you.

To make the book more challenging and more fun, many different kinds of tests are used, including sentence transformation, gap-filling, word families, multiple choice and crosswords. There is a key at the back of the book so that you can check your answers; and a word list to help you revise key vocabulary.

Vocabulary is an important part of language learning and this book will help you to develop your specialist vocabulary. When you are learning vocabulary, notice how words are used (grammar) and when they are used (context). Decide whether you only need to recognize certain items of vocabulary or whether you will actually need to use the words yourself at a later date. If you need to use words yourself, it is useful to practise making sentences of your own using the new words. The tests in this book provide a structured and systematic way for you to check what you already know, and to increase your knowledge of new concepts and terms.

Alison Pohl

The full series consists of:

Test Your Professional English: Accounting	Alison Pohl
Test Your Professional English: Business General	Steve Flinders
Test Your Professional English: Business Intermediate	Steve Flinders
Test Your Professional English: Finance	Simon Sweeney
Test Your Professional English: Hotel and Catering	Alison Pohl
Test Your Professional English: Law	Nick Brieger
Test Your Professional English: Management	Simon Sweeney
Test Your Professional English: Marketing	Simon Sweeney
Test Your Professional English: Medical	Alison Pohl
Test Your Professional English: Secretarial	Alison Pohl

1 Accounting

Fill in the missing words in the sentences below. Choose from the box. You will need to use each word more than once.

account	accounts	accountant	accounting	accountancy

1 Can you check that the figures have been entered correctly in the bank ___account___ ?

2 He's at university studying ______.

3 The management of the company have not yet decided on their ______ policies.

4 A bookkeeper writes details of financial transactions in the ______.

5 Most people in the profession read ______ magazines and journals in order to stay informed.

6 She's been working as an ______ with this firm for several years now.

7 The directors of the company approve the ______ at the end of the ______ year.

8 The chief ______ has completed the draft ______ for this year.

9 Each branch maintains its own full ______ system.

10 They have opened an ______ for the consignment to Bombay.

11 ______ is really not an exact science.

12 A business manager needs some ______ knowledge in order to understand what he reads in the company ______.

Accountancy (noun) is the theory of keeping financial records. **Accounting** (noun + adjective) refers to the activity of keeping financial records. **Account** (noun) is a record of money received and spent. **Accountant** (noun) is a person who keeps and works with financial records.

2 Introducing accounting 1

Complete the following words.

1	This company has supplied goods but has not received any money for them yet.	CREDITOR
2	Companies make this when they sell their goods for more than it costs them to make them.	PROFIT
3	Companies make this when they sell their goods for less than it costs them to make them.	LOOS
4	Goods which are bought by the company.	PURCHASES
5	Goods which the company has available to sell.	STOCK
6	An amount of money which is taken out of an account.	WITHDRAWL
7	Customers who have received goods but not paid for them yet.	DEBTORS
8	A reduction in the price which is offered to customers.	DISCOUNT
9	This is the name of the difference between the credit and debit sides of an account.	BALANCE

10	This is drawn up to check that the two sides of the accounts are the same.	T _ _ _ L B _ _ _ _ _ E
11	The cost of transporting goods is called this.	C _ _ _ _ _ G E
12	The official books for keeping accounts.	L_D _ _ _ S

Sell goods for more than it costs to make them.

3 Facts and figures

Identify which mathematical term (a–i) describes the examples (1–9).

1 74%

2 $f = \sqrt[p]{(2YV)}$

3

	000's		000's
Jan	2.4	July	3.5
Feb	2.5	Aug	4.7
Mar	3.9	Sept	6.9
April	4.6	Oct	6.3
May	3.4	Nov	6.8
June	3.6	Dec	3.4
Monthly..................			= 4.33

4 1,623 + 3,004 = 4,627

6 9,260 – 1,111 = 8,149

7 $\frac{1,505}{5} = 301$

8

Direct costs	724
Indirect costs	200
Costs	
Direct : Indirect = 3.62	

9 £12.24/hour

a formula

b multiplication

c division

d percentage

e average

f ratio

g addition

h rate

i subtraction

Notice the prepositions in the following phrases:

to add a number ***to*** *a number*

to subtract a number ***from*** *a number*

to multiply a number ***by*** *a number*

to divide a number ***by*** *a number*

4 Introducing accounting 2

Complete the following words.

1 This is the name for buildings, machinery, money in the bank and money owed by customers. ASSETS

2 The loss of value of the things in number 1. D _ P _ _ _ _ _ _ _ _ N

3 Money which is borrowed. LOAN

4 The extra money a company or person pays for borrowing money. INTEREST

5 The total sum of money which is supplied by the owners of a company to set it up. CAPITAL

6 Cash or goods which the owner takes from the company for his own private use. DRAWINGS

7 These are bought by people wishing to invest in the company. SHARES

8 The extra amount which is paid for a company above the value of its assets. GOODWILL

9 The purchase of another company. ACQUISITION

10 An official examination of the accounts. AUDIT

11 A financial plan for the future. BUDGET

12 A statement of the financial position of the company. BALANCE SHEET

5 Phrases

What are the meanings of the phrases in bold in the sentences (1–10) below? Choose the correct definition from the list (a–j) on the right. Write your answers in the grid below.

1 How do you **account for** the sudden fall in the stock value?

2 Agents buy and sell goods **on their own account**.

3 They gave the solicitor a detailed **account** of the customer's business deals in the last year.

4 The draft accounts had to be adjusted **on account of** the discovery that a major debtor had gone bankrupt.

5 Raw materials **account for** 30% of the manufacturing cost.

6 They are regular customers in this shop and are now able to buy **on account**.

7 **On no account** should these figures be released before the board meeting.

8 When making decisions for the future the managers have to **take** this year's poor performance **into account**.

a people say

b report

c under no circumstances

d consider

e explain

f big customers

g for themselves

h because of

9	**By all accounts**, they will benefit greatly if the deal goes through.	i	on credit
10	The advertising company has won two new **accounts** in South Africa.	j	represent

1	2	3	4	5	6	7	8	9	10
e									

They gave the solicitor a detailed account of the customer's business deals in the last year.

The word **account** is now used in everyday English to form phrases with different meanings, e.g. *by all accounts*, *account for*. These phrases are easier to learn and remember in short sentences.

6 Expressing change

Here are thirty verbs/verb phrases which are used to express changes. Which words could be used to decribe the change or movement in each graph? Write the phrases in the column below the appropriate graph. The number of spaces shows the number of phrases for each.

~~be stable~~	~~decline~~	decrease
deepen	descend	deteriorate
diminish	~~double~~	drop
dwindle	escalate	expand
fall	grow	hold firm
improve	increase	jump
maintain same level	recover	reduce
remain constant	retain position	rise
rocket	shrink	slow down
slump	soar	suffer

It's soaring!

A

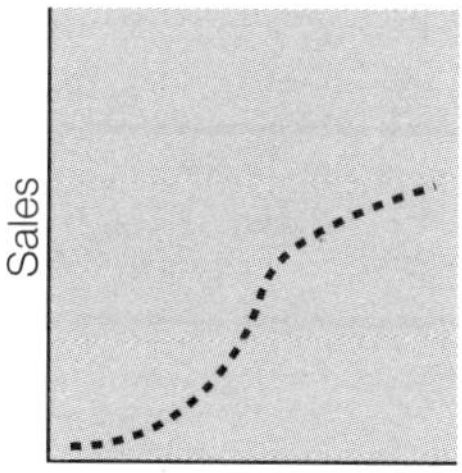

B

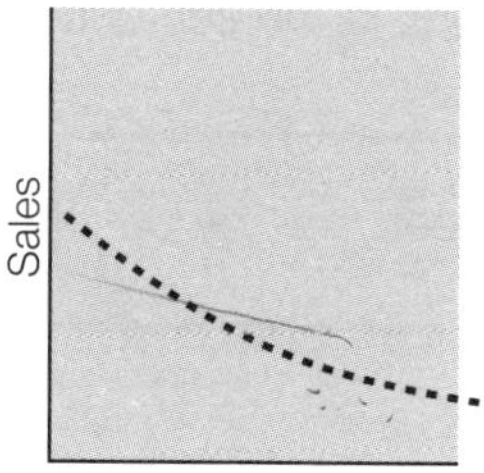

C

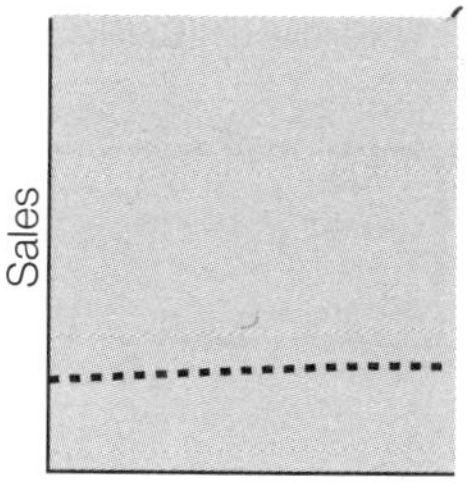

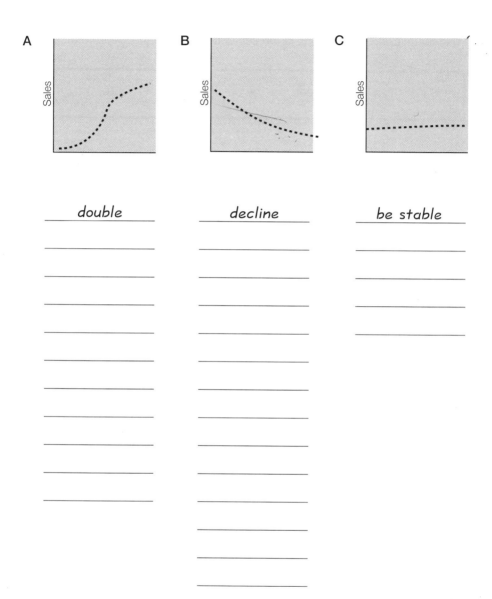

A	B	C
double	decline	be stable

Several of the verbs listed are intransitive and don't take a direct object, e.g. *fall*: Prices *fell*. *Rise* is the same, e.g. Prices *rose*. But *raise* can take an object, e.g. The company *raised prices*.

7 Prepositions of change

Fill in the missing prepositions in the sentences below. Choose from the box.

at	between	by	from	of	to

1 Labour costs have fallen ___from___ 22% of total production costs ___to___ 14% in the last ten years. That's 8%!

2 There was a dramatic fall in sales to the USA ________ 1997 and 2000.

3 The company is currently selling 20,000 units ________ £23 each.

4 The growth in sales has led to a rise ________ 30% in profits.

5 A 10% drop in sales has reduced the profit ________ 40%.

6 During 1999/2000 we increased retail floor space ________ 5% ________ a total ________ 48,000m^2.

7 They expect to create 1,450 jobs worldwide ________ the end of next year, at the latest.

8 Capital investment for the year stands ________ £6,000.

9 Pre-tax profits reached a peak ________ $5m two years ago but have been lower since.

10 Weekly sales have levelled off ________ £34,000.

11 Increased efficiency has resulted in a lowering of the break-even point from 2,770 ________ 2,500 units.

12 The rise in raw material prices is expected to be ________ 3.5% and 4.5% this year.

Using the wrong preposition could give the wrong information. Compare: *Prices rose* ***to*** *£100* and *Prices rose* ***by*** *£100*. ***To*** gives us the new level. ***By*** gives us the difference between levels.

8 Technology

Look at the drawings below and write the numbers 1–14 next to the correct word or phrase.

calculator	6	CD	9
eraser	2	fax machine	4
floppy disk	10	keyboard	13
laptop computer	3	mobile phone	7
mouse	14	pager	
paper and pencil	8	printer	5
computer monitor	1	personal computer	

9 Computing

Complete the crossword.

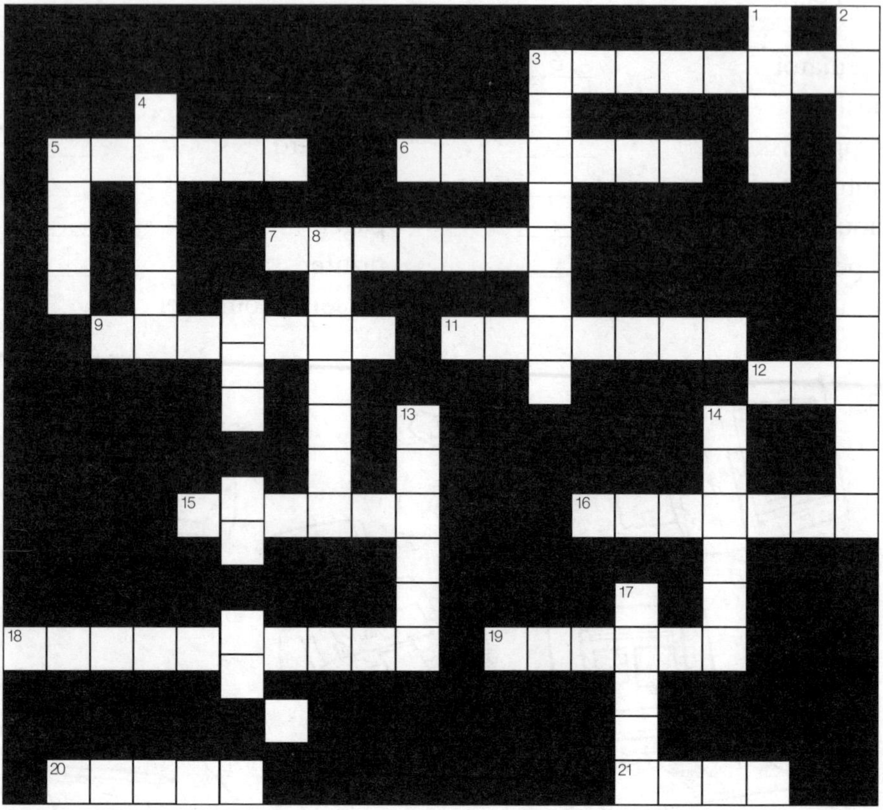

Across

3 This software system allows the user to structure the way information is stored and makes it easy to find and use this information when required.

5 The main computer when several computers are working together.

6 Send on an e-mail you have received to someone else.

7 Put in the new software programme.

9 A company on the internet has its own _________.

11 Use this to enter pictures, photos or graphs.

12 A problem in the software.

15 Do this regularly so that you don't lose important information.

16 When you're writing an e-mail you don't need to be connected to the telephone; you can work ______.

18 A document which is sent together with an e-mail.

19 While you are looking for information on the internet you work ______.

20 You will have to ______ your records if a customer or supplier changes an address, telephone number, or credit details.

21 Do this if you want to store the information.

Down

1 Information stored on the computer is called ______.

2 This will help you find the information you want on the world wide web.

3 Take information from the world wide web so you can save or print it.

4 You do this if you spend time looking on the internet.

5 Unwanted e-mails.

8 Several computers may be joined together in a ______.

10 This software package is used for working with numerical information.

13 Bring data from other sources or goods from another country!

14 Remove numbers, letters or whole text.

17 One of these in the system could destroy everything.

10 Banking

Take one word from the left-hand column and one from the right to complete each of the following sentences.

~~account~~	bank
bank (2)	book
base	cash
central	charges
cheque	code
overdraft	facility
sort	~~number~~
standing	order
withdraw	rate
	statement

1 All correspondence with the bank must include the company *account* *number* .

2 The company ________ ________ should be kept in a safe place when not being used.

3 The office needed money, so had to ________ ________ from the account.

4 Each branch of the bank has its own unique ________ ________ .

5 The bank will set ________ ________ which are payable for each transaction carried out by the bank.

6 Interest rates are calculated as a small percentage above ________ ________ .

7 The ________ ________ in Britain is the Bank of England and in Germany it's the Bundesbank.

8 The bank can be asked to pay the rent for the building automatically every month by ________ ________ .

9 The ________ ________ each month lists all the money which has gone into and out of the account.

10 The company has negotiated an ________ ________ which allows them to spend more than they actually have in the account.

Certain pairs of words are often found together, e.g. *overdraft facility*, *bank rate*. Try to learn these words as a pair. To help you remember, write the words in short sentences. You can test more pairs of words in Test 43.

11 Cash accounts

Fill in the missing words or phrases in the sentences below. Choose from the box.

authorization	batch	beneficiary	brought	carried	cleared
contra	discrepancies	~~petty cash~~	remitter	threshold	transaction

1 Small amounts of money which are paid out for things such as petrol, soap and bus fares are usually recorded in the _petty cash_ book.

2 The account which receives payment is known as the ______ while the account sending payment is the ______ .

3 Each single movement of money in the account is known as a ______ .

4 At the beginning of each month the balance from the previous month is recorded at the top of the account as ______ forward and at the end of the month as balance ______ forward.

5 The bank statement should be checked against the cash book to make sure the figures are the same and that there are no ______ .

6 When several payments are made by computer banking they are normally transmitted to the bank together in a ______ .

7 If double entry has taken place within the cash book the item does not need to be entered in another book as double entry and the item is known as a ______ .

8 When a cheque is received and paid into an account it will be debited to the account once it has been ______ .

9 Before instructions can be transmitted to the bank it is necessary to have ______ from one, two or possibly three executive officers.

10 There will normally be a maximum amount of money which can be transferred from an account and this is known as the ______ .

12 Trading account

Fill in the missing words in the document below. The first one has been done as an example. Choose from the following.

amount description dispatch date ~~invoice~~ quantity tax point
terms trade discount unit price value added tax

Joe Small Ltd
Main Industrial Estate
Anytown

INVOICE

to: N Tees Ltd
24 High Street
Newtown

(1) *invoice* No.0066798 (2) ________ 14 January 20__

Customer Account No. Tee4331 (3) ________ 12 January 20__

item no	(4) ________	(5) ________	(6) ________	(7) ________
P245	file cards	3 packs	3.50	10.50
T479	A4 paper	10 reams	2.80	28.00
AX311	pencils	5 boxes	1.20	6.00

Total goods	44.50
(8) ____________	8.90
	35.60
(9) ____________	3.56
Total	39.16

(10) ____________: 30 days net

13 Buying and selling

Choose the correct word in each of the following.

1 The book/file which contains a list of all company sales arranged by date is known as the _sales day book_ .

a) sales account b) sales card c) sales invoice (d) sales day book

2 A ______________ is not recorded in double entry.

a) cash discount b) refund c) trade discount d) cash sale

3 Faulty goods which are sent back to the supplier by the customer are known as ______________ .

a) returns b) provisions c) recovers d) discounts

4 A ______________ system should make sure that debtors do not owe too much money.

a) quality control b) credit control c) credit note d) credit transfer

5 A company sells goods on credit, but if customers never pay for these goods the money owing is known as ______________ .

a) bad debts b) debits c) bad payment d) bankrupts

6 The estimated expense of not being paid by debtors is known as a/an ______________ .

a) allowance b) devaluation c) proviso d) provision

7 If you calculate different percentages for debts which have been owing for different lengths of time, you can prepare a/an ______________ schedule of debtors.

a) progressive b) ageing c) reducing d) increasing

8 In many countries a tax is added to the price of goods and services, but some goods may be ______________ and no tax is due.

a) exempt b) exceptional c) excused d) uncovered

9 At the end of an accounting period, details of tax collected and tax paid are given to the authorities on an official form called a ______________ .

a) statement b) declaration c) return d) confirmation

14 Adjustments

Match the following examples with the correct word or phrase from the box. Write the correct number in the spaces in the box.

error of omission	3	compensating error	____
journal	____	error of commission	____
error of original entry	____	an overcast account	____
error of principle	____	reversal of entries	____
an undercast account	____		

1 Magda Glyda has added up the figures to produce a figure which is less than it should be.

2 The sales account and the purchases account were both added up wrongly by the same amount.

3 Maria Gonzalez forgot to record the transaction in the accounts.

4 Reinhardt Mann recorded the purchase of the lorry in the purchases account but it was a fixed asset.

5 Pierre Barber has corrected the error and recorded it in this book.

6 Anna Benelli made a mistake in the invoice but entered the same figure in both the sales and the customer's accounts.

7 Lesley Brunovsky entered the correct amount in the correct accounts but as a debit where it should have been a credit, and a credit where it should have been a debit.

8 Garry Blues has added up the figures wrongly to produce a total which is greater than it should be.

9 Theo Koch entered the correct amount but in the wrong customer's account.

15 Making changes

Here is a letter from a firm of accountants to a client. Complete the letter by inserting the missing phrases. Choose from the box below.

a	adjustments	f	accumulated
b	the audited accounts	g	change
c	ended 30 April 2002	h	the bank overdraft
d	do not hesitate to contact	i	cheque for £2,500
e	with the final accounts	j	provision for bad

Dear Mr Lee

We have pleasure in enclosing five copies of the full accounts for the period (1) _____c_____ .

We are also sending you a list of the adjustments which you need to make to your Nominal Ledger so that the opening balances at 1 May 2002 agree with (2) __________ .

- Please put in the details of a (3) __________ drawn in December 2001 for Customs and Excise into bank payments. These details are missing so the Nominal Ledger understates (4) __________ .
- Increase bank payments by £185.20 and code it direct to purchases. This will cover various small differences which have (5) __________ over the years.
- Make new Nominal Ledger code headings for (6) __________ debts.
- (7) __________ the present code headings for plant and equipment at cost to 0011.

We feel it is better to separate the cost and depreciation of the fixed assets in the Nominal Ledger to make it easier to compare (8) __________ . It also makes it easier to find any (9) __________ which have been made.

If you have any problems with these changes or would like to discuss them further, please (10) __________ us.

Yours sincerely

Lydia Triffs

16 Profit and loss

Fill in the missing words in the sentences below. Choose from the box.

administrative expenses	cost of sales	distribution	dividend
extraordinary	~~ordinary~~	retained	turnover

1 As AZ Designs Ltd is a small printing company, all their printing contracts are known as ___ordinary___ activities.

2 Recently, a film company paid AZ Designs a large amount of money to use the company's premises when they were making a film. This was recorded in the Profit and Loss Account as ____________ income.

3 Income which the company makes in its normal activities is known as ____________ .

4 At the end of the year, some of the profits may be shared out among the shareholders who will receive a ____________ .

5 The costs of getting the goods to the customers are shown as ____________ costs in the Profit and Loss Account.

6 Materials which are used up in manufacturing and workers' wages are recorded as ____________ .

7 The secretary's salary and expenses incurred in the office are shown as ____________ .

8 The company may decide to keep some of the profits at the end of the year and the amount is shown as ____________ profits.

For many businesses, the main reason for the accounting function is to calculate profits earned or losses incurred. The **Profit and Loss Account** is used to compare **actual results** with **projected results**, and for future planning. Organizations with a financial interest in the company will also wish to see the **P&L Account**.

17 Profit and Loss Account

Match the items (1–10) with the entries (a–j) from a Trading and Profit and Loss Account.

Trading and Profit and Loss Account

				£000's
			£	£
4	a	Turnover		900
____	b	Cost of sales		550
		Gross profit		350
____	c	Distribution costs	60	
____	d	Administrative expenses	45	105
				245
		Other operating income		55
				300
____	e	Income from shares in related companies	15	
		Income from other fixed asset investment	20	
		Other interest receivable	10	45
				345
____	f	Interest payable		18
		Profit on ordinary activities before taxation		327
____	g	Tax on profit on ordinary activities		109
		Profit on ordinary activities after taxation		218
____	h	Extraordinary income	18	
		Tax on extraordinary profit	6	
				12
		Profit for the financial year		230
		Retained profits from last year		40
				270
		Transfer to general reserve	60	
____	i	Proposed ordinary dividend	130	190
____	j	Retained profits carried to next year		80

1 The value of stock at the end of the year has been deducted to arrive at this figure.

2 Bank interest on the overdraft.

3 Dividends from investments in shares with voting rights in other companies.

4 Net invoiced amounts for sales.

5 This year's profits which will not be paid out to investors.

6 The delivery drivers' wages.

7 Money received for rent on buildings which have been let for a short time as they are not being used.

8 This money will probably be paid out to shareholders.

9 Telephone, stationery and legal fees.

10 An overprovision for corporation tax from last year.

The terms and format used in a **Trading and Profit and Loss Account** vary according to the company, the law of the country and the convention chosen. How is the P&L Account presented in your country? The one shown here is a fairly standard example from England.

18 End of year: confusing words

Look at the words in *italic* in each of the following sentences and choose the correct one.

1 On the first day of the new financial year, the company counts and records all the materials, parts, machines, stationery etc. in the annual *stockpile/stock-take*.

2 New regulations mean that the accountants must *publicize/publish* the Trading and Profit and Loss Account in one of four *formats/formations*.

3 If the information in the Trading and Profit and Loss Account is only for *insider/internal* use, the company can decide to present the information as it wishes.

4 The law states how much information must be *disclosed/enclosed* in the Trading and Profit and Loss Account.

5 This company's turnover is *descended/derived* from the sale of manufactured goods.

6 The notes which are *appended/adhered* to the Trading and Profit and Loss Account explain how the figures have been compiled.

7 The company wishes to *approximate/apportion* Motor Expenses equally between Distribution Costs and Administrative Expenses.

8 The auditors' *remuneration/compensation* for their services should be shown in the notes.

9 The accountants have to *accredit/accrue* Corporation Tax on ordinary activity profit when they are preparing the Trading and Profit and Loss Account.

10 The final tax figure will probably be different to the book figure so an amount has been transferred to the *defect/deferred* taxation account.

11 It is necessary to state the *emoluments/emollients* of the Chairman in the notes.

Once you have checked your answers try to write short sentences of your own for the two words given in each sentence. This will help you remember the difference between them. You may need a good English:English dictionary to help you. You can test more confusing words in Test 58.

19 Personal contacts

Look at the following drawings; then fill in the missing words. Choose from the following.

a Would you like a copy of the report?

b May I introduce my colleague, Mr Fry?

c Well, I really need a bit more time!

d Don't mention it! Pleased to have been able to help.

e Not completely, I'm afraid.

f Could I ask you to sign here?

g Good morning, Mr Berneike. Nice to see you again.

h Is next Friday suitable?

i Please take a seat.

j Don't worry. I'll fill them in later.

1

2

3

4

5

6

7

8

9

10

In Britain people shake hands when they meet for the first time, when they haven't met for some time and when they leave again. Colleagues at work who see each other daily don't shake hands.

20 Telephoning

Fill in the missing words in the telephone dialogue below. Choose from the box.

Can I suggest	Can you let me have	First of all	
How can I help you	I'd also like	I look forward to	
~~My name is~~	That's right	We can arrange	What we need is

Berg: Anders Berg.

Peretti: Hello. (1) My name is Ruth Peretti. I'm Managing Director of Woodtech Ltd, a wood machinery manufacturer.

Berg: Oh, yes. (2) ________________ ?

Peretti: Well, an associate in the industry recommended you. You helped raise finance for Bill Wylde a few years ago.

Berg: Yes. (3) ________________ .

Peretti: Well, Woodtech Ltd now wants to expand into new markets with a new product. Up till now we have served specialists in the wood industry but our new product is aimed at the small manufacturer. (4) ________________ finance.

Berg: Right! (5) ________________ I'll need some background information. (6) ________________ a copy of your balance sheet and profit and loss figures for the past three years?

Peretti: Of course.

Berg: (7) ________________ a letter outlining your ideas and a cash flow forecast for the new product.

Peretti: Fine.

Berg: If you let me have these by the beginning of next week, (8) ________________ a meeting for the week after. That will give me enough time to look through the figures.

Peretti: Good. (9) ________________ a meeting on Monday 16th at 9 o'clock?

Berg: That's fine. (10) ________________ receiving your letter and accounts in the next few days.

Peretti: I'll post them first thing tomorrow. I look forward to meeting you on Monday 16th.

Berg: Goodbye.

Peretti: Goodbye.

Use *This is ....* (name) to tell the listener who is calling when you expect the listener to know you. *My name is ....* (name) is only used when you are calling someone who doesn't know you. If someone calls and asks to speak to you, the reply is *Speaking!*

21 Businesses

Match the following sentences (1–11) with the words or phrases (a–k) on the following page. Write your answers in the grid below.

1 The holder of these has lent the company money but has no voting rights.

2 A group of five accountants have decided to form an association to carry on business in common and make a profit.

3 The investors give these people the power to run the company.

4 This company holds more than 50% of the voting shares in another company.

5 Members of the public can only invest in this company if they are invited to do so.

6 Investments in many companies can be made by buying shares on this market.

7 The public at large can be shareholders in this company.

8 The golf club was set up with no intention of making a profit.

9 Fifty-one per cent of the voting shares of this company are held by another company.

10 This is the meeting which is held once a year for the shareholders.

11 This exists when several companies are in a relationship of owning and being owned.

a	subsidiary	b	group
c	non-profit-making	d	stock exchange
e	partnership	f	directors
g	private limited	h	debentures
i	public limited company	j	holding company
k	annual general		

1	2	3	4	5	6	7	8	9	10	11
h										

In Britain, **Ltd** is the abbreviation used after the name of a private limited company. Only private investors can invest in this company. **Plc** is the abbreviation used after public limited companies. Members of the public can buy shares in these companies on the stock exchange.

22 False practices: world building 1

A Complete the following table.

Noun	Verb
fraud	defraud
deceit/deception	
pilfering	
	waste
misappropriation	
	break
	forge
falsification	
	err
embezzlement	

B Fill in the missing words in the sentences below. Choose from the table above.

1. When valuing the stock, there are many reasons why the manager makes an allowance of 0.5% for natural __wastage__ of items.
2. We had to make sure that employees could not ____________ small items from the office.
3. The bookkeeper tried to ____________ over £200,000 but the auditor became suspicious when he found changes to some invoices.
4. In order to avoid paying tax he decided to ____________ the documents by understating profits.
5. Several people lost large sums of money due to the ____________ of pension funds.
6. A serious ____________ was found in the draft accounts before they were published.
7. They discovered that the signature on the cheque was a ____________ .

Nouns in the table above are formed with the suffixes **-tion**, **-age**, **-ment**, or **-ery**. Can you think of some more nouns which end in this way? You can practise more word building in Tests 28, 46 and 60.

23 Shares

Fill in the missing words in the sentences below. Choose from the box.

appropriation	bonus	~~denomination~~	interim	issued	nominal
ordinary	preference	preliminary	redeemable	uncalled	

1 This company has issued shares in £5 denomination .

2 At the end of the financial year, profits are first of all allocated to pay the fixed percentage dividends on ____________ shares.

3 The ____________ shareholders have voting rights but do not have a fixed percentage dividend.

4 The company have decided to issue ____________ shares free of charge to their existing share holders.

5 The company is allowed to issue a total amount of shares known as the authorized share capital or ____________ capital. However, the ____________ capital may be less than that.

6 There were large ____________ expenses in starting the company.

7 They have only asked for some of the amount payable on the shares, so there is still a lot of ____________ capital.

8 2005/2013 written behind a debenture means that it is ____________ during that time.

9 The final accounts should include an ____________ account which shows how the company will use the profits.

10 After trading for six months, the company paid out an ____________ dividend.

24 Shares issue

A company has issued 10,000 shares and the following extract has been taken from the bank account.

Bank

	£		£
Application and Allotment		Application and Allotment refund	50
Application monies	1550		
Allotment monies	1500		
First call	3600		
Second call	2700		
H. Jay	0075		

Use the information in this extract to fill in the missing words in the text below. Choose from the box.

allotment application applications call excess first
forfeited ~~issued~~ nominal oversubscribed refund
reissued second

The company (1) issued 10,000 6% preference shares of £1 each.

Investors who wanted to buy the shares had to pay 10% on (2) __________ , 20% on allotment, 40% on the first (3) __________ and 30% on the (4) __________ call. The sale was very popular and the issue was (5) __________ . (6) __________ were received for 15,500 shares. A (7) __________ of the money for 500 shares was made. An (8) __________ was made on the basis of two shares for every three applied for, for the remaining 15,000. The (9) __________ application monies were set off against the (10) __________ monies asked for.

The holder of 1,000 shares didn't pay the (11) __________ and second calls and his shares were (12) __________ . These shares were then (13) __________ at 75% of (14) __________ value to H. Jay.

25 Partnerships

Choose the correct word or phrase in the following statements about partnerships.

1 If a partner is liable only to the amount of capital he invested he is a limited partner.
a) liability (b) limited c) corporate d) dead

2 The partners want an official agreement about their share in the partnership, so they are going to draw up a/an ______________ of partnership.
a) deed b) transaction c) title d) instrument

3 If there isn't an official written agreement, but a partner signs a balance sheet which shows that profits have not been shared equally, agreement would be ______________ .
a) implied b) stated c) drawn d) believed

4 Partners can choose to produce fixed capital accounts or ______________ capital accounts.
a) changeable b) moving c) variable d) fluctuating

5 A partner who does not take an active part in the business is called a ______________ partner.
a) silent b) dead c) sleeping d) inactive

6 When partners can't or don't want to continue in partnership there is a ______________ of the partnership.
a) divorce b) decomposition c) amalgamation d) dissolution

7 When this happens a ______________ Account is opened to record the transactions.
a) Sales b) Realization c) Distribution d) Liability

8 When the partnership comes to an end, the debts or liabilities are ______________ .
a) discharged b) disposed c) distributed d) dissolved

9 One partner, who owes the partnership money, will have to cancel his ______________ to the partnership firm.
a) deal b) claim c) indebtedness d) articles

In Britain groups of professional people such as accountants, lawyers, dentists and vets often form partnerships. Can you think of any other groups that form partnerships?

26 Giving advice

The following phrases are from two different letters: a letter to a firm of accountants asking for advice and the reply. They are all mixed up. Put them in the correct order to produce two correct letters.

1 We look forward to hearing from you.

Yours sincerely

Ian Blest

2 Thank you for your letter of 26 January regarding the setting up of a partnership. I am now writing to give you my first thoughts which you may want to discuss further.

3 So far we have agreed that Mr Ford will give £20,000 as capital but will not take part in the running of the business. Mr Grant will manage the business but contribute only £3,000. Mr Blest will provide £8,000 as capital and assist in the business if and when required.

4 I trust that you will find these points useful. If you wish to discuss anything further please let me know.

5 Dear Mr Blest

6 Yours sincerely

Camilla Simone

7 Turning to profit sharing, I think it would be best for each of the partners to receive interest on their capital investment and then decide how to share the remaining profits.

8 First of all, I suggest that as Mr Ford is not going to be involved in the daily management of the partnership he be made a limited partner. This means that his liability is limited to the amount of capital invested by him. He can receive a fixed amount of interest on his investment or an amount based on the profits. I feel that Mr Grant, as the managing partner, and Mr Blest who will be actively involved, should receive salaries for their work.

9 Dear Ms Simone

10 We now need financial advice about the structure of the partnership and would be grateful if you would assist us. We have planned our next meeting for 21 February, and would like to discuss your ideas then.

11 Two friends and myself have discussed setting up a partnership and we are now writing to you for advice.

12 Finally, the law does not require you to draw up a legal deed of partnership but I think you should have a written agreement.

request for advice

9				

reply

When a letter begins with the name of the recipient, e.g. *Dear Ms Simone*, it can end with **Yours sincerely**, **Best wishes** or **Kind regards** but not with **Yours faithfully**. *Yours faithfully* is only used when the letter begins *Dear Sir/Madam* or *Dear Sirs*.

27 Acquisitions

Look at the following drawings, then fill in the captions. Choose from the following.

- a joint venture
- b a take-over bid
- c showing interest in another company
- d launching a bid
- e consolidated accounts
- f a financial honeymoon
- g minority interest
- h agreeing the book value of assets

1 ___c___

2 ________

MEGA CORP INC
WE WANT TO BUY

3 ________

NOTHING TO PAY FOR SIX MONTHS
NOTHING TO PAY FOR SIX MONTHS

4 ________

GLENDALE POWER STATION & GENERAL ELECTRICIT

5 ________

6 ________

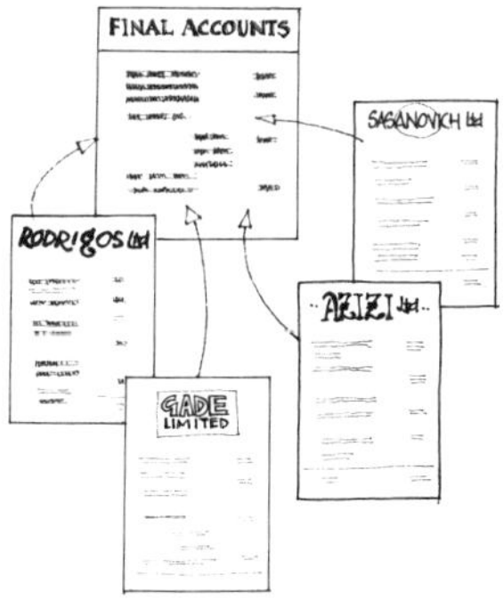
FINAL ACCOUNTS
SAGANOVICH Ltd
RODRIGOS Ltd
AZIZI Ltd
GADE LIMITED

7 ________

8 ________

28 Earnings: word building 2

Use the words in **bold** to form a word which fits in the blank space.

1	Wages are earnings which are calculated and paid weekly .	**WEEK**
2	The payroll contains details of all the ____________ who work for the company.	**EMPLOY**
3	The employer makes a ____________ for tax from the workers' gross salary.	**DEDUCT**
4	When calculating how much tax to pay, personal ____________ is set against the amount someone earns.	**RELIEVE**
5	In the UK, people who have worked and paid into National Insurance can claim benefits from the State. These include ____________ benefit and a pension for ____________ .	**EMPLOY** **RETIRE**
6	To provide for their old age, people may pay monthly ____________ to a pension scheme.	**CONTRIBUTE**
7	Payments to a pension scheme may be tax ____________ .	**DEDUCT**
8	Pension schemes operated by a company may be non-____________ .	**CONTRIBUTE**

9 The law in some countries says that an employee who is ill should get a certain amount of pay which is known as ____________ sick pay. **STATUTE**

10 In some companies the employees have a holiday ____________ of 20 days. **ENTITLE**

11 They receive an increase each year as they are paid an ____________ salary. **INCREMENT**

12 The government sets the tax band ____________ between one tax threshold and the next. **WIDE**

The law in some countries says that an employee who is ill should get a certain amount of pay which is known as ____________ sick pay.

The adjectives in this exercise are formed with the suffixes **-ly**, **-ible**, **-ory**, **-al**. Can you think of some more adjectives which end in the same way? Tests 22, 46 and 60 also test word building.

29 Taxes

Match each definition on the right with a term from the box. Write the term beside each definition.

capital gains tax   corporation tax
creative accounting   excise duty   ~~income tax~~   loophole
money laundering   progressive tax   tax deductable   tax evasion
tax haven   tax loss   tax shelter   value added tax

1 *income tax* People pay this tax on the money they earn.

2 ________________ Companies pay this tax on their profits.

3 ________________ Profits from the sale of assets may be subject to this tax.

4 ________________ Government tax on things such as cigarettes, alcohol and petrol.

5 ________________ This kind of tax means that the more money you earn, the higher the rate of tax you have to pay.

Tax haven

6 ________________ A clever but still legal way of reducing the amount of tax to an absolute minimum.

7 ________________ A country such as Liechtenstein and the Bahamas where tax is low.

8 ________________ A mistake in the law which allows people to avoid paying tax.

9 ________________ These payments are not subject to tax.

10 ________________ In the accounts the company is seen to make this if capital expenditure is brought forward to use up profits.

11 ________________ This tax is added to the price of goods and services.

12 ________________ Avoiding paying tax by giving false information to the authorities.

13 ________________ Investment schemes which allow people to postpone paying tax.

14 ________________ Handling money made from illegal activity.

Creative accounting

30 Taxation

The following phrases are from three different letters written by an accountant concerning tax matters. They are all mixed up. Put them in the correct order to produce three correct letters.

1. Yours sincerely
M D Tippet
The Tippet Partnership

2. We notice from our files that your 2001 Income Tax return has not been completed yet.

3. Yours faithfully
M D Tippet
The Tippet Partnership
Enc.

4. We would recommend that you make payments on account of £2.345 on 1 January 2002 and £2,346 on 1 July to avoid interest charges.

5. Dear Sir/Madam

6. Dear Mr Pendergast

7. We also enclose the Corporation Tax return and trust that you will be able to agree our figures in due course.

8. Dear Ms Post
We have recently received a copy of your 2000/2001 tax assessment. As this is incorrect we have lodged a Notice of Appeal.

9. On behalf of Collins Enterprises Ltd we enclose a copy of the financial accounts for the year ended 30 March 2001 together with a copy of our Corporation Tax computation.

10. We would like to complete it and would be grateful if you could let us have the details of dividends received from your UK shareholdings for the year ended 5 April 2001.
Yours sincerely
M D Tippet
The Tippet Partnership

letter 1			letter 2				letter 3		
6					7		8		

31 Depreciation

Circle the **odd one out** in each of the following.

1 Fixed assets could include

a) buildings b) plant and machinery
c) the firm's delivery vans (d) fuel for the vans

2 Depreciation due to physical deterioration of an asset may include

a) wear and tear b) theft c) erosion d) rot

3 Machinery becomes obsolete due to

a) new technology b) consumption
c) changes in production methods d) changes in fashion

4 Amortization is the provision for consumption of the following items

a) mortgages b) leases c) patents d) copyright

5 A provision for depletion would be used for the following items

a) mines b) buildings c) quarries d) oil wells

6 The following are methods of depreciation

a) straight-line b) reducing balance
c) the sum of the year's digits d) market value

7 A machine could be disposed of by being

a) scrapped b) resold c) revalued d) traded in

8 The accounts which would record the sale or disposal of a machine are

a) machinery account
b) sales account
c) machinery disposals account
d) provision for depreciation (machinery) account

In Britain land and buildings are expected to increase in value over time but for accounting purposes they must be depreciated in the accounts. Is the situation similar in your country?

32 Depreciating: phrasal verbs

Replace the words in brackets in each of the following sentences with a phrasal verb of similar meaning. Choose from the following and make any necessary changes.

carry on	catch on	clear up	close off	draw up	go over
look up	sell off	set aside	set out	turn out	~~write off~~

1 As the machine had no scrap value, they simply (recorded as worthless) __wrote__ it __off__ .

2 The methods used for depreciating the fixed assets should be (displayed) ____________ in the notes at the end.

3 Despite massive losses this year, the firm intends to (continue) ____________ trading.

4 They found the true value of the land when the firm had to (dispose of) ____________ it ____________ .

5 We think it is best to (keep available) ____________ money each year for future investment in new equipment.

6 The estimated life of the assets (proved) ____________ to be very accurate.

7 If you cannot remember the formula for the reducing balance method of depreciation, (find in a book) ____________ it ____________ .

8 It's a good idea to (consider) __________ the different ways of depreciating assets before deciding on one particular method.

9 After disposal of the asset you can (finish) __________ the account.

10 The surplus or deficiency is transferred when you (prepare) __________ the Profit and Loss Account.

11 The sum of the year's digits method of depreciation is beginning to (become popular) __________ in Europe now.

12 A change in the method of depreciation should (solve) __________ the problem of allocating costs.

Phrasal verbs consist of a verb together with a preposition or an adverb. There are two possible word orders for phrasal verbs containing an adverb: verb-pronoun/noun-adverb or verb-adverb-noun

write it/the machine **off**	**write off** the machine
clear it/the problem **up**	**clear up** the problem
sell it/the land **off**	**sell off** the land
look it/the formula **up**	**look up** the formula

33 The work of the auditor: prepositional phases

Fill in the missing prepositional phrases in the following sentences. Choose from the box.

agree with	blame for	caused by	~~difference between~~	in line with
insist on	reason for	refer to	responsible for	suspicious of

1 The auditor discovered that there was a *difference between* the cash book and the bank balance.

2 If the entries in the accounts are not clear, he can ______________ the original invoices.

3 You must ______________ an official signature on all large orders.

4 The auditor must check that the records are ______________ the company requirements.

5 The auditor must ask the ______________ any large discounts or allowances.

6 The auditor is ______________ checking the reason for any changes in the accounts.

7 The authorities will ______________ the auditor ______________ any mistakes in the accounts.

8 The auditor must check that the purchase invoices ______________ the entries in the Purchases Journal.

9 The auditor should be ______________ any short-cut methods of correcting errors.

10 Mistakes may be ______________ the wrong steps used in the original accounting process.

34 Auditing

Match the following terms (1–14) with the correct definition (a–n) on the right and write your answers in the grid below.

1	statutory audit	a	official document stating the internal rules of the company
2	continuous audit	b	following one after the other without a break
3	Memorandum of Association	c	this checks that controls are operating effectively
4	Articles of Association	d	required by law
5	walk through test	e	money received from one debtor is wrongly recorded to another
6	compliance test	f	regulates the company's relationship with the public
7	substantive test	g	testing a small number of representative items
8	teeming and lading	h	carried out all the time
9	auditor	i	following documents or transactions through the system
10	prior period	j	piece of work you are given to do
11	audit assignment	k	careful study of all the details
12	corroborate	l	accountant who examines a firm's accounts
13	statistical sampling	m	previous length of time
14	consecutive numbers	n	make sure it's true with more information

1	2	3	4	5	6	7	8	9	10	11	12	13	14
d													

The word audit is pronounced /ˈɔːdɪt/, the same vowel sound as draw /ɔː/ and not /aʊ/ as in out.

35 Ratios 1

Complete the following words.

1	The profit expressed as a fraction or percentage of the cost price.	M A R K - U P
2	The profit expressed as a fraction or percentage of the selling price.	M A _ _ _ _
3	A percentage of profits which they pay the manager.	C _ _ _ _ _ _ ION
4	Ratios help us to analyze and ___________ accounting information.	INT _ _ _ _ _ _
5	Shows that a firm has enough money to survive in the short term.	LI _ _ _D _ _ _
6	How quickly stock is turned over.	STOCK _ _ _ _
7	The range of different types of goods which a firm sells.	S A _ _ _ M_ _
8	The sales figure minus any goods which are returned.	T_ _N _ _ _ R
9	Shows if the firm can meet its debts in the long term.	S_ _V _ _ _ Y
10	The amount of borrowing by a firm.	G_ _R _ _G
11	The rate of return on an investment in shares.	Y _ _ _ D
12	Expenses which do not change even when activities are increasing or decreasing.	F _ _ _ D
13	Expenses which change when the firm's activities change.	V A R _ _ _ _ E
14	You can see this when information from several years is compared.	T R _ _ D

36 Ratios 2

A Match the type of ratio (a–e) with the correct description of its function (1–5).

1 shows how well the business can meet its commitments as they fall due

2 shows how successfully the business is trading

3 shows how well the business is using its assets

4 provides information about how the capital structure of the firm is affecting the cost of capital and the return to shareholders

5 shows how the company's performance is reflected in the market price of a share

a capital structure

b liquidity

c investment

d profitability

e use of assets

B Which type of ratio are the following? Choose from a–e above.

- current ratio ____
- price earnings ratio ____
- fixed assets/net worth ____
- asset/sales ____
- acid test ratio ____
- gross profit/sales ____
- dividend cover for ordinary shares ____
- borrowing/net worth ____
- collection period for debtors ____
- net profit after tax/sales ____

37 The Balance Sheet

Fill in the missing entries in the Balance Sheet below. Choose from the following.

Amounts owed by related companies	Called up share capital
Creditors: amounts falling due after one year	~~Development costs~~
Fixtures and fittings	General reserve
Net current assets	Profit and loss account
Stock	Tangible assets

	£000's		
	£	£	£
Fixed Assets			
Intangible Assets			
(1) Development costs	180		
Goodwill	40	220	
(2) ______			
Land and buildings	600		
(3) ______	20	620	
Investments			
Shares in related companies	4,100		
Loans to related companies	59	4,159	4,999
Current Assets			
(4) ______			
Raw materials	600		
Finished goods	800	1,400	
Debtors			
Trade debtors	1,200		
(5) ______	400		
Called up share capital not paid	500		
Prepayments	400	2,500	

		£000's	
	£	£	£
Creditors: amounts falling due within one year			
Debentures	600		
Bank overdrafts	50		
Bills of exchange payable	50	700	
(6) ____________________			3,200
Total assets less current liabilities			8,199
(7) ____________________			
Debentures	100		
Bank loans	100	200	
			7,999
Capital and reserves			
(8) ____________________			6,000
Other reserves:			
Capital redemption reserve	300		
(9) ____________________	599	899	
(10) ____________________			1,100
			7,999

In the Balance Sheet you may see different terms used:
stock = inventories, debtors = receivables, creditors = payables.

38 Valuation of stock

Complete the following words.

1	The first goods which come in are the first to leave the firm. (abbreviation)	F I F O
2	Goods leaving the firm are the last which were received. (abbreviation)	L _ _ _
3	The value of all the goods in stock is calculated as an average.	A _ _ _ _ _ _ C _ _ _
4	The direct cost of production (materials, labour and expenses) give this figure.	P _ _ _ _ COST
5	If a stock item were sold, this is the money which would be received after taking away the costs of disposal.	NET R_ _L _ _ _ _ _ E VALUE
6	The cost of getting an item to take the place of a stock item.	R_ _L _ _ _ M_N_ COST
7	The value of items which a company is producing at the moment.	W _ _ _-IN-P_ _ _ _ _ SS
8	Items which are used up when producing goods for sale.	R_ _ M _ _ _ _ IALS
9	The main valuation method used in calculating the input value.	HIS _ _ _ _ _ COST
10	A retailer can return unsold goods to the manufacturer when they are supplied on these terms.	S _ _ E OR RET _ _ _
11	The quantity of goods which are available for sale.	S T _ _ _ L _ _ _ L

39 Goodwill

A Look at the following drawings which depict different reasons for paying for goodwill, then fill in the captions. Choose from the following.

- **a** Costs in research and development
- **b** The business enjoys a monopoly
- **c** Trade marks and patents
- **d** Skilled labour force
- **e** A well-known name
- **f** Negative goodwill
- **g** Location of the premises

1 ____________________

2 ____________________

3 ____________________

4 ____________________

5 ____________________

6 ______________________ 7 ______________________

B Goodwill may be treated in different ways in the accounts. Fill in the missing words in the sentences below. Choose from the following.

acquired	amortized	balance sheet	brought	created
eliminated	reserves	useful		

In the company's books:

Purchased goodwill should normally be (1) _____________ immediately as an asset from the books when it is (2) _____________ . In some companies, it may be appropriate for purchased goodwill to be (3) _____________ year by year over its (4) _____________ economic life. Goodwill which has been (5) _____________ within the company and not bought, should never be (6) _____________ into the books at all. When there is negative goodwill, it should be added to the (7) _____________ in the (8) _____________ of the firm.

40 Accounting policy

The following extracts are taken from Notes to the Accounts. Give a more formal word or phrase for the words given in brackets. Choose from the words in the box at the start of each section.

adjustments	applicable	compliance	~~convention~~	stating

Basis of preparation of accounts

The accounts have been prepared under the historic cost (normal practice) (1) convention, as modified by the revaluation of certain fixed assets, in (agreement) (2) ________ with the provisions of the Companies Act 1985 and (fitting) (3) ________ to UK Accounting Standards. The group accounts are the result of the consolidation of the accounts of the company and its subsidiaries, with appropriate (changes) (4) ________ .

Rationalization and closure costs

Continued rationalization costs are charged before (giving) (5) ________ the trading profit. Closure costs of major sites are treated as an extraordinary item.

arising	estimated	excess	is incurred	per annum

Depreciation

Depreciation on freehold buildings and leaseholds with more than 50 years unexpired is provided on a straight-line basis at 3% (each year) (6) ________ . No depreciation is provided on freehold land. Computers and other equipment are depreciated on a straight-line basis over their (guessed) (7) ________ lives of between four and ten years.

Goodwill

Goodwill (existing) (8) ________________ on acquisitions, being the (extra) (9) ________________ of cost over the fair value of the net assets acquired, is charged against reserves in the year of acquisition.

Research and development expenditure

All revenue expenditure is charged against profits in the year in which it (happens) (10) ________________ .

considered	existing	in respect of	projected	ruling

Foreign currencies

Assets and liabilities in foreign currencies are expressed in sterling at exchange rates (given) (11) ________________ at the balance sheet date.

Pensions

Contributions are made to pension schemes to provide for retirement benefits related to (forecast) (12) ________________ final salaries in respect of (today's) (13) ________________ staff, and for post retirement increases in pensions, and are charged to the profit and loss account as incurred.

Deferred taxation

Deferred taxation arises (for) (14) ________________ items where there is a timing difference between their treatment for accounting purposes and their treatment for taxation purposes. Provisions are made at the appropriate rates for deferred taxation to the extent that it is (thought) (15) ________________ the liability or asset will arise in the foreseeable future.

41 Funds

Choose the correct answer in each of the following.

1 Funds coming into a firm are known as _sources_ of funds.

a) springs
b) sources
c) origination
d) income

2 The ways these funds are used are known as the ______________ of funds.

a) application
b) delegation
c) disposal
d) consumption

3 ______________ funds include money in our hands and in the bank.

a) working
b) current
c) profit
d) cash

4 When you take away current liabilities from current assets you have the amount of ______________ funds.

a) liability
b) working capital
c) asset
d) flow

5 Financial statements about cash funds are usually known as ______________ statements.

a) cash flow
b) cash resource
c) cash outflow
d) cash loss

6 An item which doesn't involve flow of funds is ______________ .

a) sale of fixed asset
b) drawings
c) depreciation
d) loan repayment

7 An item which involves flow of funds is _____________ .

a) provision for bad debts
b) book loss on sale of fixed asset
c) sale of fixed asset
d) book profit on sale of fixed asset

---

8 After making adjustments for items which don't involve the flow of funds the net profit or loss is known as _____________ .

a) gross profit
b) outflow of funds
c) cash movements
d) total generated from operations

---

9 If a company reduces their stock and the number of debtors, they will _____________ cash.

a) deliver
b) release
c) discharge
d) liberate

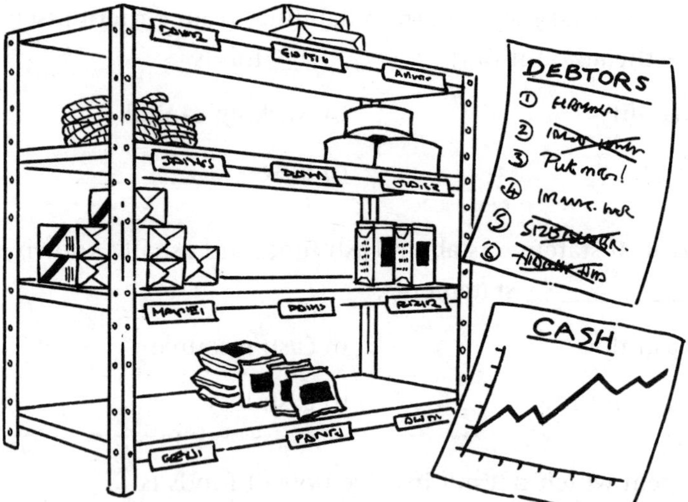

When the words **debt** and **debtor** are spoken the letter 'b' is silent. /dɛt/, /'dɛtə/.

42 Costs

Fill in the missing words in the terms below. Choose from the box.

apportionment centre conversion ~~direct~~ fixed integrated indirect interlocking labour marginal

Term		Definition
1	*direct* costs	Costs which are directly related to making a product (e.g. materials, labour and expenses).
2	________ costs	Costs of changing materials into products.
3	________ costs	Costs which are not directly related to making a product, e.g. rent, administration.
4	costs ________	This could be a location, a function, a piece of equipment or a group of employees where you can identify and allocate costs for control purposes.
5	costs ________	You divide the common overhead costs between the various activities which use them according to how much they use.
6	________ costs	Costs which always stay the same even if the number of items produced changes.
7	________ costs	The cost of paying workers to make the product.
8	________ cost	The cost of making a single extra unit above the number already planned.
9	________ cost accounts	You don't separate financial and cost accounting.
10	________ cost accounts	Separate cost and financial accounts which are reconciled sometimes.

43 Cost analysis

Take one word from the left-hand column and one from the right to complete each of the following sentences.

~~financial~~	facilities
prime	analysis
functional	decisions
consumable	process
maximum	~~data~~
business	profit
arbitrary	materials
manufacturing	cost

1 Accountancy provides _financial_ _data_ which is used to make future business decisions.

2 In order to succeed, company managers try to make __________ __________ because this is where capital growth comes from.

3 Because accountants rely on estimates rather than 'true costs', they often have to make __________ __________ .

4 __________ __________ are used up in the manufacturing process but are not part of the final product.

5 All the direct costs of manufacturing are referred to as __________ __________ .

6 Overhead is the cost of providing ___________ ___________ which you need to produce goods.

7 The management accountant should understand the ___________ ___________ used to make a product in the factory.

8 Cost accounting uses ___________ ___________ which looks at where each transaction comes from.

The management accountant should understand the ___________ used to make a product in the factory.

Remember that words are often used in association with other words depending on the context. Try to note words which often go together. You could do this in spider diagrams similar to the idea in Test 45

44 Manufacturing costs

A Which of the following manufacturing steps is being described below?

assembly	dispatch	finishing	maintenance
material handling	material storage	packing	production set-up
production	purchasing	quality control	~~sourcing~~

1 finding suppliers ______ sourcing

2 buying ______

3 receiving and moving materials ______

4 providing space and the necessary conditions for keeping materials ______

5 preparing machines for manufacture ______

6 keeping the machines in working order ______

7 making products ______

8 putting the products together ______

9 applying a protective cover to the product ______

10 checking to make sure the product reaches the correct standard ______

11 putting products in boxes and crates ______

12 transporting the finished products ______

B Fill in the missing words in the sentences below. Choose from the following.

appropriate	cost driver	overhead	overstate	selling

Costing methods are used to decide product ______ prices and profitability. ______ costs are charged to products. A mistake in the method of calculating could ______ the cost of the product. The activity costing method means allocating the ______ share of activities to each product. A factor which influences the cost of an activity is known as a ______ and is used to calculate how much should be apportioned to each product.

45 Stock costs

Here are 20 costs related to holding stock, obtaining stock and stockout. Decide which cost group they belong to and write them in the spider diagram on the next page.

accounting costs air-conditioning for warehouse damage
deterioration extra costs for urgent purchases inventory costs
interest on capital invested in stock loss of customers
loss of customer goodwill lost sale pilfering
production stoppages purchasing department costs
setting-up costs for production run stores' insurance and security
stores' running costs tooling costs for internal ordering
transport costs wages for stores' staff workforce frustration

Sally and George were mystified by their loss of customers.

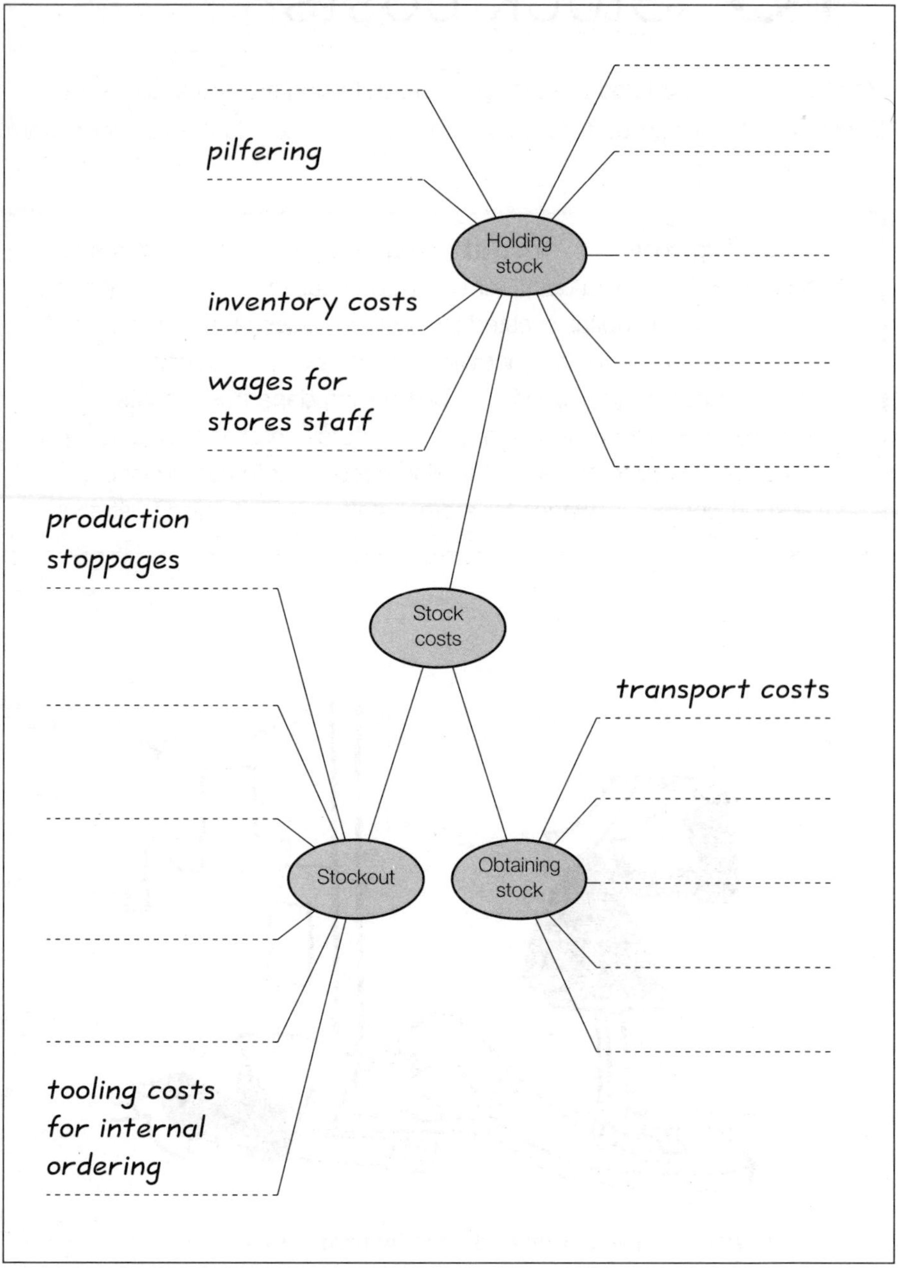

This is one way to organize your vocabulary. Putting vocabulary into topic or subject groups means you can add new words as you meet them.

46 Cost ascertainment: word building 3

Use the words in **bold** at the end of each of the following sentences to form a word which fits in the blank space.

1	It's not always possible to calculate product costs of multiple products _accurately_ .	**ACCURATE**
2	You need product costs to make a ____________ between products.	**COMPARE**
3	Management may wish to expand the sales of the more ____________ products.	**PROFIT**
4	Process costing looks at the ____________ of costs in a department over a period of time.	**ACCUMULATE**
5	Operating costing is the way of calculating the cost of the ____________ of services.	**PROVIDE**
6	Material losses which result from the nature of the operating method are usually not ____________ .	**AVOID**
7	Losses caused by inefficient operations are ____________ .	**PREVENT**
8	The disposal of waste might incur ____________.	**EXPEND**
9	Some costs may be ____________ by the sale of scrap.	**RECOVER**
10	Bookkeepers normally don't make a ____________ between scrap and waste.	**DISTINCT**
11	____________ may be possible on some products which fail quality control.	**RECTIFY**
12	In jobbing production there is usually no ____________ in design from previous orders.	**REPEAT**

You can practise more word building in Tests 22 and 28 and 60.

47 Marginal costing

A Which cost behaviour pattern is illustrated in each of the graphs shown?

semi-variable costs 4

curvi-linear variable costs ______

total fixed costs ______

mainly variable costs ______

total linear variable costs ______

mainly fixed costs ______

stepped costs ______

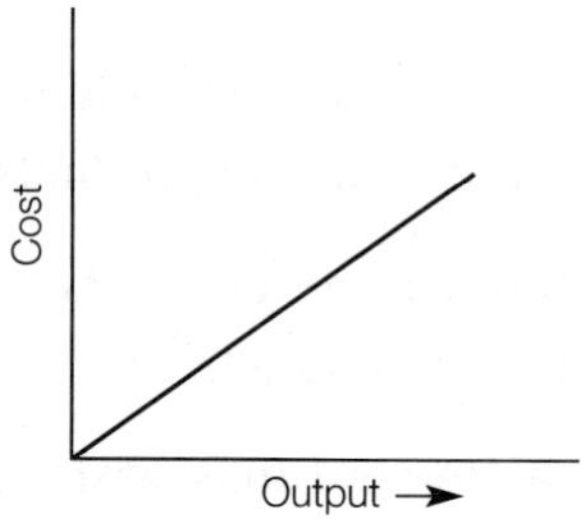

1

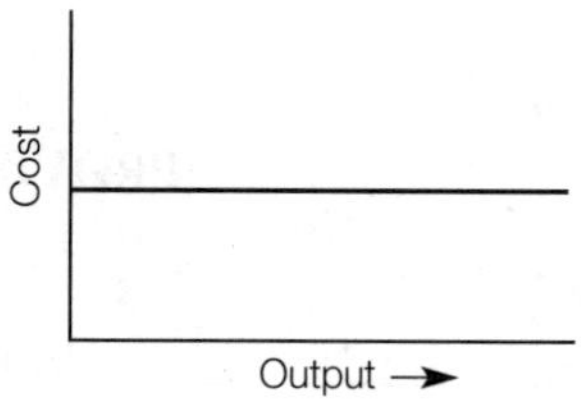

2

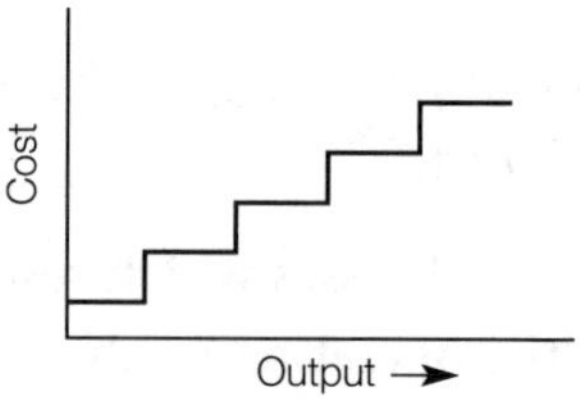

3

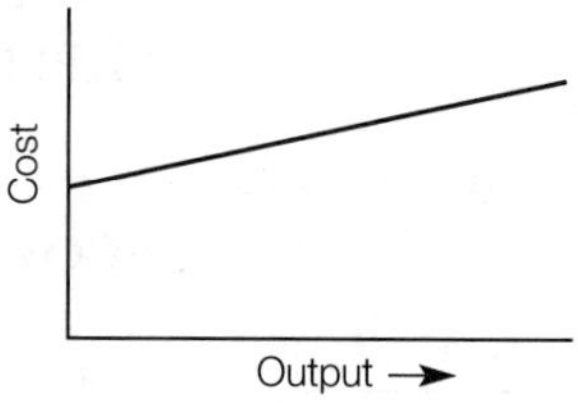

4

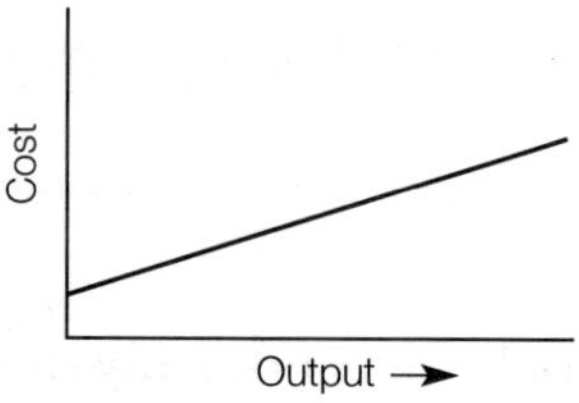

5

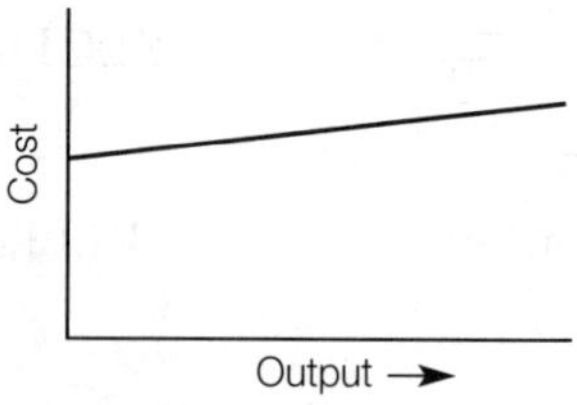

6

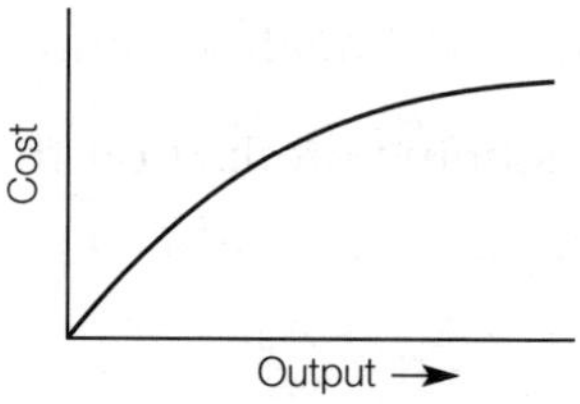

7

B Which graph represents the following overhead cost items?

a One supervisor is required for eight workers on the production floor, so the costs for supervisors' salaries increase with each eight workers.

b Waste disposal costs per unit fall as output rises showing an economy of scale.

c Royalties are paid on each unit produced.

d The production manager receives a small basic salary and a percentage commission on each item produced.

e There is a quarterly standing charge for the telephone and additional costs for each call made.

f There is a standard charge for the machine and normal usage but usage above the agreed volume increases per unit.

g The rent for the buildings remains the same whether output increases or decreases.

Royalties are paid on each unit produced.

48 Company expansion: formal verbs

Choose a more formal verb from the box to replace the words in brackets in the following sentences.

~~absorb~~	boost	concentrate	cover	gain	generate	hold
identify	implement	map out	penetrate	pinpoint	reach	reduce
set	strengthen	submit				

1 We will have to ___absorb___ (deal with) an increase in material costs because we don't want to increase our selling price.

2 Increased domestic sales should ______________ (make) more profit this year.

3 The manager went to the meeting to ______________ (present) his financial plan for the expansion.

4 The increased profit must be enough to ______________ (pay for) the operating and financial expenses.

5 Careful production costing should enable us to ______________ (find) loss-making products and ______________ (explain exactly) the reasons for the problem.

6 The sales target has been ______________ (decided) for the next six months.

7 It's the company's aim to ______________ (get) a bigger market share.

8 Everyone will have to work hard to ______________ (get to) the planned business targets.

9 The plan is to _____________ (cut) sales of the loss-making products and _____________ (give attention to) on those which are more profitable.

10 We will _____________ (put into action) expansion plans early next year.

11 The plan is to _____________ (get into) the North African market and _____________ (increase) sales of the main products.

12 At the same time we will have to _____________ (keep the same) the present selling price in the domestic market.

13 Every effort will be made to _____________ (make better) our position in the market.

14 They have set up a project group to _____________ (layout in detail) an expansion strategy.

The plan is to get into the North African market.

49 New markets: prepositions 2

Fill in the missing prepositions in the sentences below. Choose from the box.

on	for	in	to	of

1 The directors are interested __in__ the prospects of future developments in South America.

2 At the meeting they will decide ______ financial targets for the next six months.

3 We look forward ______ receiving a detailed plan of the project.

4 The director gave a brief account ______ the company's recent performance.

5 Future dividends will depend ______ the success of the new product.

6 The director stressed the importance ______ effective control on spending.

7 The marketing strategy is to concentrate ______ developing markets in Europe.

8 There is a need ______ a full risk assessment before going into these markets.

9 We must be aware ______ the attitude towards foreign investors.

10 There may be difficulties ______ enforcing contracts.

11 For the site construction we will rely _______ local contractors.

12 We have already reached agreement _______ local short-term credit.

13 It is necessary _______ everyone involved in the project to show respect _______ local customs.

14 We are proud _______ recent successes in these markets.

15 The sale of the building has been agreed subject _______ contract.

16 We are all involved _______ finding solutions to the current problems.

Certain nouns, verbs and adjectives combine with specific prepositions. It is important to learn the preposition together with the word. For example, to have an effect **on**, to decide **on**, to be interested **in**.

50 Planning information

Rearrange the letters to form the correct word for each of the following.

1 Where customers demand low prices, employees expect high wages and shareholders want high dividends, there is a c*onflict* of i*nterest* (fltcconi fo terinest).

2 The corporate plan will normally be either production, market or profit o__________ (ontedrie).

3 A business cannot stand still, it must either grow or decline and so a net cash flow increase is the growth t__________ (rgetta).

4 Corporate planning must plan several years ahead so l__________ r__________ f__________ (ongl genra castforinge) is a major part of corporate planning.

5 Managers use m__________ (odmngeill)to predict the future under different conditions.

6 We sometimes see similar changes every four, five or six years; this is known as a c__________ p__________ (licalcyc pttaern).

7 When movements in an organization follow a similar pattern to other events they show c__________ (catorrionel).

8 To form a corporate policy, corporate planning looks at every aspect of company activity and this is known as a t__________ c__________ (talto cepcont).

9 Changes in the population structure or age profiles of customers are examples of d__________ (graphmodeic) information.

10 Information about economic conditions will include forecasts for growth, GDP and i__________ (ionintfla).

51 Budgeting

Fill in the missing words in the sentences below by making combinations with the word *budget*. In some expressions *budget* appears as the second word. Choose from the following.

appropriation	cash	~~committee~~	current	fixed	functional
master	officer	period	principal	selling	

1 Next year's budget is being prepared by the ___budget___ ___committee___ over the next few weeks.

2 They haven't taken variable output levels into account and have set a ________ ________ of £800,000 for raw materials.

3 The sales manager has to give his budget estimate to the ________ ________ by tomorrow morning so that he can check it before the meeting next week.

4 For most companies the ________ ________ is a year but due to the rapidly changing nature of the fashion industry they prepare their budget every four months.

5 There is a limit to the amount of money which may be spent on research and development, so an ________ ________ has been prepared.

6 In order to have an effective management control system, we prepare a ________ ________ for a short period of time.

7 The market demand is for 900,000 units, but the existing plant, which is only capable of producing 500,000 units, is the ________ ________ factor.

8 The marketing department is divided into ten territories, each with its own ________________ ________________ .

9 Sales reps' salaries, rent for sales offices, advertising and publicity are some of the items included in the ________________ ________________ .

10 In order to make sure that there will be enough cash available to meet demands and provide additional finance if required, a ________________ ________________ must be prepared.

11 The budgeted profit and loss account is incorporated in the final ________________ ________________ once the board of directors has agreed it.

52 Variances

A Delete the wrong word in italics in the following two sentences.

1 The difference between the budgeted and actual results is ***adverse /favourable*** when profits are higher.

2 The difference between the budgeted and actual results is ***adverse /favourable*** when profits are lower.

B In the following situations decide if the variances are favourable (F) or adverse (A).

1 Three hundred tonnes of materials were used at a price of $45 per tonne. The standard price is $47 per tonne. _____

2 The company bought salt at standard price but the process used more than planned. _____

3 The workers worked harder than expected during the year and production increased. _____

4 The budgeted expenditure on overhead was £50,000. The actual overhead was £65,000. _____

5 The chemicals used in the process were used in different proportions from the standard mix and the total price was lower. _____

6 One member of the manufacturing team was away from work without wages but the team worked equally well without him. _____

C Match each of the situations (1–6) above with the correct variance (a–f) below.

a overhead expenditure variance _____

b material usage variance _____

c material price variance _____

d materials mix variance _____

e labour mixture variance _____

f labour efficiency variance _____

53 Control

Complete the following words.

1 This type of accounting is used to measure how effective a manager's decision has been. R E S P O N S I B I L I T Y

2 This is the first of three steps in a formal control system. S_ TT _ _ _

3 This is the second of three steps in a formal control system where the objectives are put into action. OP _ _ _ _ ING

4 The last of three steps in a formal control system where the results are studied. F _ _ _ _ ACK

5 This means correct and containing no mistakes. A C _ _ _ _ _ E

6 A difference to the expected standard. VA _ _ _ _ CE

7 To give responsibility to other people in the organization rather than do it yourself. D _ _ _ _ ATE

8 This kind of system accepts that standards can be changed and adjusted as necessary. O P _ _ - LO O _ _D

9 Products do this if they reach the required quality. C _ _ _ _ RM

10 To change or reset standards. R _ _ ISE

11 This data allows you to compare alternatives. C _ _ _ AR _ _ IVE

12 This system works towards an ideal standard. C L _ _ _D – LO O _ _D

13 At present, at the moment, today's. C _ _ _ _ N _

14 Only information which is important and significant. R _ _ _ V _ NT

15 An instrument which reacts to certain conditions and provides information. S _ _ S _ R

16 To change, alter or adapt. M _ _ _ FY

54 Performance: phrasal verbs 2

A Match the following phrasal verbs with a synonym on the right.

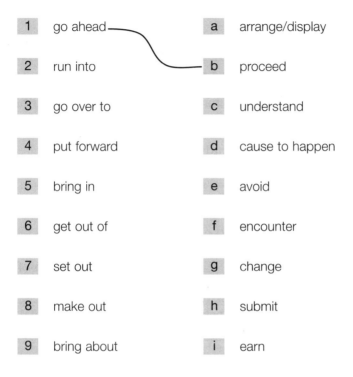

1	go ahead	a	arrange/display
2	run into	b	proceed
3	go over to	c	understand
4	put forward	d	cause to happen
5	bring in	e	avoid
6	get out of	f	encounter
7	set out	g	change
8	make out	h	submit
9	bring about	i	earn

B Fill in the missing phrasal verbs in the sentences below. Choose from the list (1–9) above.

1 The increase in raw material prices will ________________ a reduction in profits.

2 The contract to refit the cruise liner will ________________ much needed revenue.

3 Include all the relevant figures on the performance report and then _______________ it _______________ for senior management.

4 The company have _______________ problems of setting realistic budgets because they have a poor accounting system.

5 The department managers have to _______________ their budgets by the end of this week.

6 Because of incomplete records, it is impossible to _______________ how the final figures were calculated.

7 It's amazing what some firms will do to _______________ paying corporate tax.

8 Profits over the last three years have increased steadily and the firm has decided to _______________ with the expansion of the business.

9 Because of large variances between the budgeted and actual costs, they should _______________ a different method of calculating the variance.

Remember that a preposition or adverb together with a verb may give that verb a specific meaning. Phrasal verbs are often more informal and are seldom used in formal documentation.

55 Break-even analysis

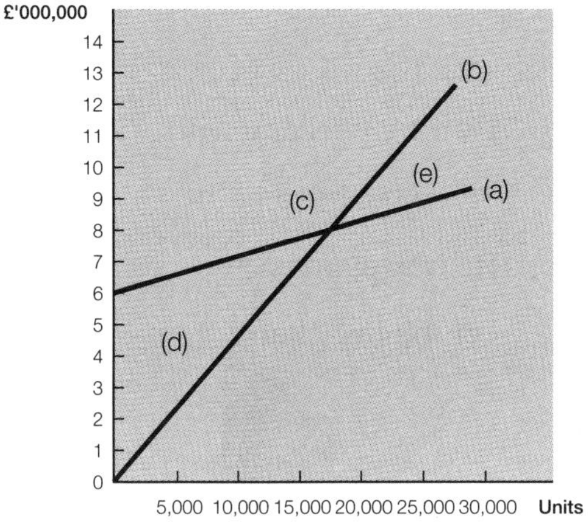

Graph A

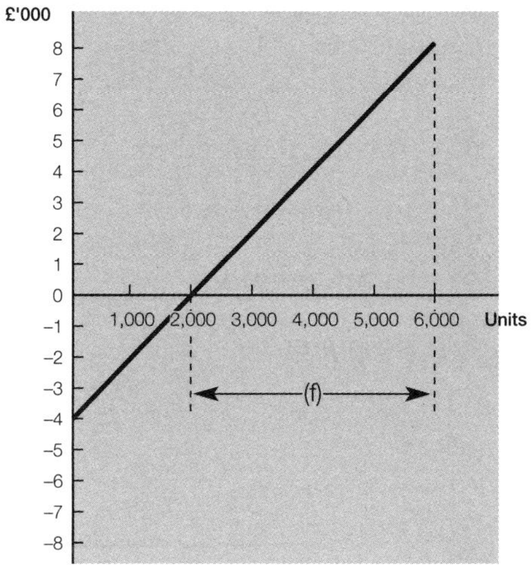

Graph B

1 What do the lines (a) and (b) in graph A represent?

a) T _ _ _ _ C _ _ _ b) S _ _ _ _

What is point (c) called? c) _ _ _ _ _ - _ _ _ _ POINT

What do areas (d) and (e) represent?

d) _ _ _ _ e) _ _ _ _ _ _

2 What is area (f) in graph B known as?

M _ _ _ _ _ OF S _ _ _ _ _

3 How much are fixed expenses per annum in graph A? ______________

4 How much are the fixed expenses in B?

5 Which graph is a basic profit graph? ______________

56 Presenting the results

Look at the following drawings; then fill in the missing words. Choose from the following.

- a You are required to
- b In other words
- c In my opinion
- d I'd prefer
- e I strongly recommend
- f There seems to be
- g He is supported by
- h Let me just clarify

1

The Law
. . . declare all sources and application of funds.

2

$250,000
+$519,000
$796,000
. . . a small mistake in the calculation.

3

£200,000
£B/E=FS/S-V
. . . how we arrived at this figure of £200,000.

4

5

6

7

8

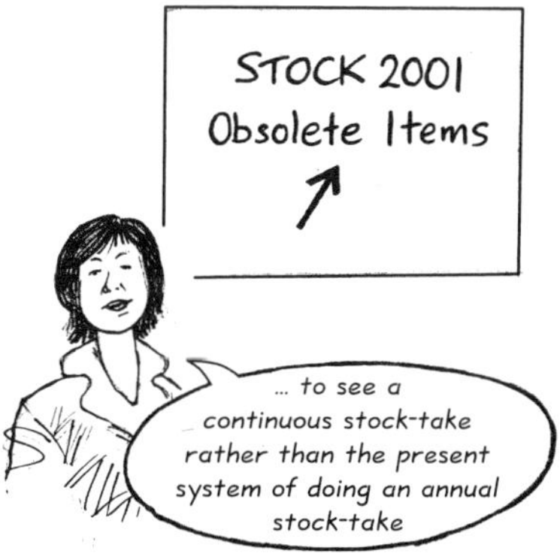

Research has shown that what is seen during a presentation has a far greater impact than what is said. What are the implications of this for speakers?

57 Pricing

Fill in the missing words in the sentences below. Choose from the box.

behaviour	ceiling	competitors	~~demand~~	discretion	elasticity
floor	full cost	leader	legislation	make or buy	substitutes

1. For some products, such as perfume, expensive and attractive packaging can increase the _demand_ for them.
2. Most businesses are in competition with other companies who manufacture similar products or ____________ .
3. A manufacturer should first look at the prices set by his ____________ before he sets his own prices.
4. When preparing information for pricing decisions, the accountant should be aware of market ____________ .
5. If sales representatives are working in a very competitive market, they should perhaps set prices at their own ____________ .
6. If the design of a product is confidential there will be no choice in the ____________ decision.
7. Government ____________ regulates the prices for certain products.
8. The maximum and minimum prices which can be set for a product are known as the price ____________ and price ____________ respectively.
9. To add a certain mark-up to the total cost of a product, a system of ____________ pricing is used.
10. A price ____________ is a product which all other companies watch when setting their prices.
11. The ____________ of demand shows how consumers will react when prices are altered.

58 Confusing words 2

Look at the words in italic in each of the following sentences and choose the correct one.

1 We're setting all the prices for next year *except/~~accept~~* the new range which won't be ready for another three months.

2 Can you *remember/remind* him to bring the comparative costs.

3 After the confusion over the bank transaction, they have agreed to *waive/wave* charges.

4 These two companies have been in *collision/collusion* with each other to fix prices.

5 We should use an *alternative/alternate* pricing structure to the one we use now.

6 We've had an *officious/official* letter to tell us about the changes in export regulations.

7 When deciding on new prices you mustn't lose *sight/site* of market behaviour.

8 Once they have agreed the figures we can *precede/proceed* with the costing.

9 Please *insure/ensure* that only the most recent figures are included in the calculations.

10 When we are setting standards we allow 10% for *deficient/ defective* goods.

11 There must be a mistake in the calculations somewhere. These figures are just not *credible/creditable.*

12 The cash budget must take *seasonal/seasonable* variations into consideration.

13 The consultant is being *prosecuted/persecuted* for tax evasion.

14 The management have now decided what *measurements/measures* to take to increase productivity.

You can test more confusing words in Test 18.

59 Investment

The same word is missing in each of the following sets of three sentences. Choose from the box.

capital ~~earnings~~ forecasts pay-back return

1 *earnings*

- The estimated ________ potential is very important when you are choosing an investment project.
- This project will yield ________ of £800,000 over five years.
- The amount of money an employee receives, and the money generated from an investment project are both known as ________ .

2 ________

- They want to know the expected ________ on investment.
- Some projects will be rejected because they do not yield a high rate of ________ .
- The ________ on an investment is the profit you get from it.

3 ________

- The ________ expenditure in the canteen, sports centre and staff room will benefit the whole company.
- In ten years we should be able to recover the ________ invested.
- The total amount of money which is invested by the owners of a company is known as ________ .

4 ________________

- What is the ________________ period of this investment likely to be?
- They'll have to be prepared to wait longer for a ________________ from this investment.
- Recovering the costs of an investment is known as ________________ .

5 ________________

- ________________ of future inflation rates have not been taken into consideration.
- The actual economic life of the assets turned out to be longer than the original ________________ .
- Statements about what is expected in the future are ________________ .

They want to know the expected ______________ *on investment.*

60 Decisions: word building 4

Complete the following words by choosing an appropriate prefix. (Some prefixes may be used more than once.) Choose from the box.

ir-	un-	in-	dis-	ab-	under-	mis-	de-

1 Low demand for their products has made production very _un_profitable.

2 We don't have a detailed cost analysis yet, so the management are ____decided about future investment.

3 You must make everything very clear now in order to avoid any ____understandings later.

4 Four Seasons Ltd has been ____successful in marketing the new product.

5 Since ____regulation, telephone companies have been able to set their own prices.

6 The company would be more profitable if they could reduce the amount of ____used capacity.

7 They have decided to ____continue the production of Product P because sales have fallen.

8 They have changed the way they measure profit as absorption costing is ____adequate.

9 The management think that the policy of expanding sales is ____correct.

10 Prices for raw materials are ____normally high at the moment.

11 They ____estimated the effect of the competitor's products on sales in this market sector.

12 The report showed that moving the production to a new site was ____desirable.

13 An increase in the price of land was totally ____expected.

14 Lots of the documentation which was lost in the fire is ____replaceable.

Prices of raw materials are abnormal at the moment.

Many prefixes make a word negative while other prefixes have a special meaning. **Mis**- = wrongly; **de**- = remove; **under**- = not enough. Can you think of some more words which begin with the prefixes given in the box above? Tests 22, 28 and 46 also test word building.

Answers

Test 1

1 account
2 accountancy
3 accounting
4 accounts
5 accountancy
6 accountant
7 accounts, accounting
8 accountant, accounts
9 accounting
10 account
11 accountancy
12 accounting, accounts

Test 2

1	creditor	7	debtors
2	profit	8	discount
3	loss	9	balance
4	purchases	10	trial balance
5	stock	11	carriage
6	withdrawal	12	ledgers

Test 3

1	d	6	i
2	a	7	c
3	e	8	f
4	g	9	h
5	b		

Test 4

1	assets	7	shares
2	depreciation	8	goodwill
3	loan	9	acquisition
4	interest	10	audit
5	capital	11	budget
6	drawings	12	balance sheet

Test 5

1	e	6	i
2	g	7	c
3	b	8	d
4	h	9	a
5	j	10	f

Test 6

A double, escalate, expand, grow, increase, improve, jump, recover, rise, rocket, soar

B decline, decrease, deepen, descend, deteriorate, diminish, drop, dwindle, fall, reduce, shrink, slow down, slump, suffer

C be stable
hold firm
maintain same level
remain constant
retain position

Test 7

1	from, to	7	by
2	between	8	at
3	at	9	of
4	of	10	at
5	by	11	to
6	by, to, of	12	between

Test 8

calculator 6
eraser 2 (also called a rubber)
floppy disk 10
laptop computer 3
mouse 14
paper and pencil 8
computer monitor 1
CD 9
fax machine 4
keyboard 13
mobile phone 7
pager 11
printer 5
personal computer 12

Test 9

Across

3 database
5 server
6 forward
7 install
9 website
11 scanner
12 bug
15 backup
16 offline
18 attachment
19 online
20 update
21 save

Down

1 data
2 search engine
3 download
4 browse
5 spam
8 network
10 spreadsheet
13 import
14 delete
17 virus

Test 10

1 account number
2 cheque book
3 withdraw cash
4 sort code
5 bank charges
6 base rate
7 central bank
8 standing order
9 bank statement
10 overdraft facility

Test 11

1 petty cash
2 beneficiary, remitter
3 transaction
4 brought, carried
5 discrepancies
6 batch
7 contra
8 cleared
9 authorization
10 threshold

Test 12

1 invoice
2 tax point (May also be invoice date.)
3 dispatch date
4 description
5 quantity
6 unit price
7 amount (Sometimes called value or total.)
8 trade discount
9 value added tax
10 terms

Test 13

1 d) sales day book (also known as sales journal)
2 c) trade discount
3 a) returns
4 b) credit control
5 a) bad debts
6 d) provision
7 b) ageing
8 a) exempt
9 c) return

Test 14

1 an undercast account
2 compensating error
3 error of ommission
4 error of principle
5 journal
6 error of original entry
7 reversal of entries
8 an overcast account
9 error of commission

Test 15

1 c
2 b
3 i
4 h
5 f
6 j
7 g
8 e
9 a
10 d

Test 16

1 ordinary
2 extraordinary
3 turnover
4 dividend
5 distribution
6 cost of sales
7 administrative expenses
8 retained

Test 17

a 4
b 1
c 6
d 9
e 3
f 2
g 10
h 7
i 8
j 5

Test 18

1 stock-take
2 publish, formats
3 internal
4 disclosed
5 derived
6 appended
7 apportion
8 remuneration
9 accrue
10 deferred
11 emoluments

Test 19

1 g	6 a
2 b	7 e
3 i	8 c
4 f	9 h
5 j	10 d

Test 20

1 My name is
2 How can I help you
3 That's right
4 What we need is
5 First of all
6 Can you let me have
7 I'd also like
8 we can arrange
9 Can I suggest
10 I look forward to

Test 21

1 h	2 e	3 f
4 j	5 g	6 d
7 i	8 c	9 a
10 k	11 b	

Test 22

A

Noun	*Verb*
fraud	defraud
deceit/deception	deceive
pilfering	pilfer
wastage	waste
misappropriation	misappropriate
breakage	break
forgery	forge
falsification	falsify
error	err
embezzlement	embezzle

B

1 wastage	5 misappropriation
2 pilfer	6 error
3 embezzle	7 forgery
4 falsify	

Test 23

1 denomination
2 preference
3 ordinary
4 bonus
5 nominal, issued
6 preliminary
7 uncalled
8 redeemable
9 appropriation
10 interim

Test 24

1 issued	8 allotment
2 application	9 excess
3 call	10 allotment
4 second	11 first
5 oversubscribed	12 forfeited
6 applications	13 reissued
7 refund	14 nominal

Test 25

1 b) limited
2 a) deed
3 a) implied
4 d) fluctuating
5 c) sleeping
6 d) dissolution
7 b) Realization
8 a) discharged
9 c) indebtedness

Test 26

request for advice: 9, 11, 3, 10, 1
reply: 5, 2, 8, 7, 12, 4, 6

Test 27

1 c	5 a
2 b	6 h
3 d	7 e
4 f	8 g

Test 28

1 weekly
2 employees
3 deduction
4 relief
5 unemployment, retirement
6 contributions
7 deductible
8 non-contributory
9 statutory
10 entitlement
11 incremental
12 widths

Test 29

1 Income tax
2 corporation tax
3 capital gains tax
4 excise duty
5 progressive tax
6 creative accounting
7 tax haven
8 loophole
9 tax deductable
10 tax loss
11 value added tax
12 tax evasion
13 tax shelter
14 money laundering

Test 30

letter 1: 6, 2, 10
letter 2: 5, 9, 7, 3
letter 3: 8, 4, 1

Test 31

1 d) fuel for the vans: this changes and is a cost to the business.
2 b) theft: deterioration is a gradual loss in value. Theft is total.
3 b) consumption: obsolete machines still exist but consumed materials are used up.
4 a) mortgages: amortization refers to intangible assets, a mortgage is a liability.
5 b) buildings: depleted items become smaller.
6 d) market value: the price an asset could be sold for today.
7 c) revalued: given a new estimate of its value.
8 b) sales account: records sales of goods produced by the firm, not assets.

Test 32

1 wrote off	7 look up
2 set out	8 go over
3 carry on	9 close off
4 sell off	10 draw up
5 set aside	11 catch on
6 turned out	12 clear up

Test 33

1 difference between
2 refer to
3 insist on
4 in line with
5 reason for
6 responsible for
7 blame for
8 agree with
9 suspicious of
10 caused by

Test 34

1 d	2 h	3 f
4 a	5 i	6 c
7 k	8 e	9 l
10 m	11 j	12 n
13 g	14 b	

Test 35

1 mark-up	8 turnover
2 margin	9 solvency
3 commission	10 gearing
4 interpret	11 yield
5 liquidity	12 fixed
6 stockturn	13 variable
7 sales mix	14 trend

Test 36

A 1 b 2 d 3 e 4 a 5 c

B current ratio (b)
price earnings ratio (c)
fixed assets/net worth (a)
asset/sales (e)
acid test ratio (b)
gross profit/sales (d)
dividend cover for ordinary shares (c)
borrowing/net worth (a)
collection period for debtors (e)
net profit after tax/sales (d)

Test 37

1 Development costs
2 Tangible assets
3 Fixtures and fittings
4 Stock
5 Amounts owed by related companies
6 Net current assets
7 Creditors: amounts falling due after one year
8 Called up share capital
9 General reserve
10 Profit and loss account

Test 38

1 FIFO (first in, first out)
2 LIFO (last in, first out)
3 average cost
4 prime cost
5 net realizable value
6 replacement cost
7 work-in-progress
8 raw materials
9 historic cost
10 sale or return
11 stock level

Test 39

A 1 e 2 b 3 d 4 c
5 g 6 a 7 f

B 1 eliminated
2 acquired
3 amortized
4 useful
5 created
6 brought
7 reserves
8 balance sheet

Test 40

1 convention
2 compliance
3 applicable
4 adjustments
5 stating
6 per annum
7 estimated
8 arising
9 excess
10 is incurred
11 ruling
12 projected
13 existing
14 in respect of
15 considered

Test 41

1 b) sources
2 a) application
3 d) cash
4 b) working capital
5 a) cash flow
6 c) depreciation
7 c) sale of fixed asset
8 d) total generated from operations
9 b) release

Test 42

1 direct
2 conversion
3 indirect
4 centre
5 apportionment
6 fixed
7 labour
8 marginal
9 integrated
10 interlocking

Test 43

1 financial data
2 maximum profit
3 arbitrary decisions
4 consumable materials
5 prime cost
6 business facilities
7 manufacturing process
8 functional analysis

Test 44

A 1 sourcing
2 purchasing
3 material handling
4 material storage
5 production set-up
6 maintenance
7 production
8 assembly
9 finishing
10 quality control
11 packing
12 dispatch

B selling
overhead
overstate
appropriate
cost driver

Test 45

holding stock
wages for stores' staff
inventory costs
pilfering
stores' insurance and security
interest on capital invested in stock
air conditioning for warehouse
deterioration
damage
stores' running costs
obtaining stock
transport costs
setting-up costs for production run
accounting costs
purchasing department costs
tooling costs for internal ordering
stockout
production stoppages
loss of customer goodwill
extra costs for urgent purchases
lost sale
work-force frustration
loss of customers

Test 46

1 accurately
2 comparison
3 profitable
4 accumulation
5 provision
6 avoidable
7 preventable
8 expenditure
9 recoverable/recovered
10 distinction
11 rectification
12 repetition

Test 47

A semi-variable costs 4
curvi-linear variable costs 7
total fixed costs 2
mainly variable costs 5
total linear variable costs 1
mainly fixed costs 6
stepped costs 3

B a 3 b 7 c 1 d 5
e 4 f 6 g 2

Test 48

1 absorb
2 generate
3 submit
4 cover
5 identify, pinpoint
6 set
7 gain
8 reach
9 reduce, concentrate
10 implement
11 penetrate, boost
12 hold
13 strengthen
14 map out

Test 49

1	in	6	of	11	on
2	on	7	on	12	on
3	to	8	for	13	for, for
4	of	9	of	14	of
5	on	10	in	15	to
				16	in

Test 50

1 conflict of interest
2 oriented
3 target
4 long range forecasting
5 modelling
6 cyclical pattern
7 correlation
8 total concept
9 demographic
10 inflation

Test 51

1 budget committee
2 fixed budget
3 budget officer
4 budget period
5 appropriation budget
6 current budget
7 principal budget
8 functional budget
9 selling budget
10 cash budget
11 master budget

Test 52

A 1 favourable 2 adverse

B 1 F	2 A	3 F
4 A	5 F	6 F
C a 4	b 2	c 1
d 5	e 6	f 3

Test 53

1 responsibility	9 conform
2 setting	10 revise
3 operating	11 comparative
4 feedback	12 closed-looped
5 accurate	13 current
6 variance	14 relevant
7 delegate	15 sensor
8 open-looped	16 modify

Test 54

A
1 go ahead b) proceed
2 run into f) encounter
3 go over to g) change
4 put forward h) submit
5 bring in i) earn
6 get out of c) avoid
7 set out a) arrange/display
8 make out c) understand
9 bring about d) cause to happen

B

1 bring about	6 make out
2 bring in	7 get out of
3 set out	8 go ahead
4 run into	9 go over to
5 put forward	

Test 55

1 a) total cost
b) sales
c) break-even point
d) loss
e) profit
2 f) margin of safety
3 £6,000,000
4 £4,000
5 Graph B

Test 56

1 a You are required to
2 f There seems to be
3 h Let me just clarify
4 b In other words
5 e I strongly recommend
6 c In my opinion
7 g He is supported by
8 d I'd prefer

Test 57

1 demand	7 legislation
2 substitutes	8 ceiling, floor
3 competitors	9 full cost
4 behaviour	10 leader
5 discretion	11 elasticity
6 make or buy	

Test 58

1 except	8 proceed
2 remind	9 ensure
3 waive	10 defective
4 collusion	11 credible
5 alternative	12 seasonal
6 official	13 prosecuted
7 sight	14 measures

Test 59

1 earnings
2 return
3 capital
4 pay-back
5 forecasts

Test 60

1 unprofitable
2 undecided
3 misunderstandings
4 unsuccessful
5 deregulation
6 unused
7 discontinue
8 inadequate
9 incorrect
10 abnormally
11 underestimated
12 undesirable
13 unexpected
14 irreplaceable

Word list

The numbers after the entries are the tests in which they appear.